VPJournals
TRAVEL JOURNAL
VPJournals

Travel Journal

Belize

VPJournals

ISBN-13: 978-1518858246
ISBN-10: 1518858244

Contact Details

Name:

Email address:

Tel:

Address:

Important Medical Information

Blood type:

Medication:

CONTENTS

Hi, I hope you enjoy this journal. It is packed with cool stuff and recommendations for you trip to Belize, and has plenty of space to record details of your trip.

Have fun in Belize

Great Places to visit in Belize

Actun Tunichil Muknal	✓
Xunantunich Mayan Ruins	
Barton Creek Caves	
Placencia	
Corozal District	
Thousand Foot Falls	
Dangriga	
Hopkins	
Caye Chapel	
Cayo District	
Shipstern Nature Reserve	

Cerros	
Turneffe Island Atoll	
Belize Glovers Reef	
Lighthouse Reef Belize	
The Great Blue Hole	
El Caracol	
Ambergris Caye Resort	
Caye Caulker	
Tobacco Caye	
South Water Caye	
Cockscomb Basin Wildlife Sanctuary	
Tapir Mountain Nature Reserve	

Cool Places to visit with Kids

Crooked Tree Wildlife Sanctuary	✓
Community Baboon Sanctuary	
Caves Branch	
Orange Walk	
Corozal History Museum	
Old Belize	
Cayo District	
Xunantunich	
Gales Point Wildlife Sanctuary	
Hol Chan Marine Reserve (Snorkelling)	
Ramon's Village	

Wahoo's Lounge, see the Chicken Drop Game	
The Split in Caye Caulker	
Lalas Bird Sanctuary, Ambegris Caye	
Butterfly Jungle	
Caye Chapel and snorkeling at Shark Ray Alley	
Belize History Center at St. George's Caye	
Swallow's Caye	
Halfmoon Caye Bird Sanctuary	
Belize Zoo	
Chocolate Tour in Toledo	
La Milpa	

Good Places to Eat in Belize

Maya Beach Hotel	✓
Sunbreeze Hotel	
Rojo Lounge	
Femi's Coffee Shop	
Dande's Frozen Custard and Sorbet	
Marian's Bayview	
The French Connection	
Red Ginger	
Habaneros	
Rojo Lounge	
Pier Lounge Bar	

Casa Picasso	
Palmilla	
Elvi's Kitchen	
Wet Lizard	
Harbour View	
Cenie's Deli	
Wild Mango	
Chon Saan Place	
Sumathi Indian Restaurant	
Nerie's II	
Celebrity Restaurants	
Hidden Treasure Restaurant	

Best Websites to Research Further

Do some more research on the internet to plan your trip:

Travelbelize.org
Belizeadventure.ca
hotguidebelize.com
Anywhere.com/belize
Know-belize.com
Belizelogue.com
Belize.com
lonelyplanet.com/Belize
wikitravel.org/en/Belize
nomadicmatt.com/travel-guides/Belize-travel-tips/

More places I want to visit on our trip

1. ______________________________

2. ______________________________

3. ______________________________

4. ______________________________

5. ______________________________

6. ______________________________

7. ______________________________

8. ______________________________

9. ______________________________

10. ______________________________

11. ______________________________

12. ______________________________

13. ______________________________

14. ______________________________

15. ______________________________

Postcard List

Name:

Address:

Name:

Address:

Name:

Address:

Name:
Address:

Name:
Address:

Name:
Address:

Name:
Address:

Name:

Address:

Name:

Address:

Name:

Address:

Name:

Address:

Name:

Address:

Name:

Address:

Name:

Address:

Packing List

✓	This Journal
	Tickets
	Passport
	Money
	Chargers
	Batteries
	Book to read
	Camera
	Tablet
	Sun glasses
	Sun cream

	Toiletries
	Water
	Watch
	Snacks
	Umbrella
	Towel
	Guide book
	Kindle
	Jacket
	Medication
	Add more below

Belize Facts

- Belize is such as small country that it is just 70 miles wide and 250 miles from top to bottom. You can get around to all the major Belize attractions without having to spend much time traveling

- The Great Blue Hole of Belize measures 1,000 feet across and reaches a depth of 400 feet

- Chicle, which was the original base for chewing gum, was a major industry in Ambergris Caye

- It was hippie backpackers who were credited with "discovering" Caye Caulker as a travel destination in the 1960's

- Thousand Foot Falls is the tallest waterfall in Belize and Central America measuring 1,600 ft. tall

- Orange Walk is often referred to as "Sugah City" due to unmistakable aroma of sugarcane filling the air

- The Cockscomb Basin Wildlife Sanctuary is one of the biggest, protected destinations in Belize and the first wilderness sanctuary for the jaguar

- Belize is the only country in Central America whose official language is English

- Mestizos have become the largest ethnic group and Belize now has more native Spanish speakers than English or Creole speakers, despite English being the official language

- Belize was formally known as British Honduras. “Belize” was adopted as the country’s name only in 1973

- The original capital of Belize is not Belmopan but Belize City

- There are over 400 islands in Belize known as cayes, running 300 kilometers off its coast

- The Canaa temple which stands 143 feet tall and built by the Mayans around 1000AD is still the tallest building in Belize

Clothes & Shoe Sizes

Children's Shoe Sizes

UK	EUROPE	US	Japan
4	20	4½ or 5	12 ½
4 ½	21	5 or 5½	13
5	21 or 22	5½ or 6	13 ½
5 ½	22	6	13½ or 14
6	23	6½ or 7	14 or 14½
6 ½	23 or 24	7 ½	14½ or 15
7	24	7½ or 8	15
7 ½	25	8 or 9	15 ½
8	25 or 26	8½ or 9	16
8 ½	26	9½	16 ½
9	27	9½ or 10	16 ½ or 17
10	28	10½ or 11	17 ½
10½ or 11	29	11½ or 12	18
11 ½	30	12½	18 or 18 ½
12	31	13	19 or 19 ½
12 ½	31	13 or 13½	19 ½ or 20
13	32	1	20
13 ½	32 ½	1 ½	20 ½
1	33	1½ or 2	21
2	34	2½ or 3	22

Children's Clothing Sizes

UK	EUROPE	US	Australia
12m	80cm	12-18m	12m
18m	80-86cm	18-24m	18m
24m	86-92cm	23-24m	2
2-3	92-98cm	2T	3
3-4	98-104cm	4T	4
3-5	104-110cm	5	5
5-6	110-116cm	6	6
6-7	116-122cm	6X-7	7
7-8	122-128cm	7 to 8	8
8-9	128-134cm	9 to 10	9
9-10	134-140cm	10	10
10-11	140-146cm	11	11
11-12	146-152cm	14	12

Women's Shoe Sizes

UK	EUROPE	US	Japan
3	35 ½	5	22 ½
3 ½	36	5 ½	23
4	37	6	23
4 ½	37 ½	6 ½	23 ½
5	38	7	24
5 ½	39	7 ½	24
6	39 ½	8	24 ½
6 ½	40	8 ½	25
7	41	9 ½	25 ½
7 ½	41 ½	10	26
8	42	10 ½	26 ½

Women's Clothes Sizes

UK	US	Japan	France / Spain	Germany	Belize	Australia
6/8	6	7-9	36	34	40	8
10	8	9-11	38	36	42	10
12	10	11-13	40	38	44	12
14	12	13-15	42	39	46	14
16	14	15-17	44	40	48	16
18	16	17-19	46	42	50	18
20	18	19-21	48	44	52	20

Men's Shoe Sizes

UK	EUROPE	US	Japan
6	38 ½	6 ½	24 ½
6 ½	39	7	25
7	40	7 ½	25 ½
7 ½	41	8	26
8	42	8 ½	27 ½
8 ½	43	9	27 ½
9	43 ½	9 ½	28
9 ½	44	10	28 ½
10	44	10 ½	28 ½
10 ½	44 ½	11	29
11	45	12	29 ½

Men's Suit / Coat / Sweater Sizes

UK / US / Aus	EU / Japan	General
32	42	Small
34	44	Small
36	46	Small
38	48	Medium
40	50	Large
42	52	Large
44	54	Extra Large
46	56	Extra Large

Men's Pants / Trouser Sizes (Waist)

UK / US	Europe
32	81 cm
34	86 cm
36	91 cm
38	97 cm
40	102 cm
42	107 cm

We have included another copy of this at the back of the book, so you can find it quickly again when you are in Belize

Belize Trip Diary

Write a daily diary during your trip

Day 1

Date: ____________ **Weather:** ____________

Day 2

Date: ______________ **Weather:** ______________

Day 3

Date: ____________________ **Weather:** ____________________

Day 4

Date: ____________ **Weather:** ____________

Day 5

Tip! Send your postcards

Date: ____________ **Weather:** ____________

Day 6

Date: ______________ **Weather:** ______________

Day 7

Date: ____________ **Weather:** ____________

Day 8

Date: ______________ **Weather:** ______________

Day 9

Date: ____________ **Weather:** ____________

Day 10

Date: ________________ **Weather:** ________________

Day 11

Date: ____________________ **Weather:** ____________________

Day 12

Date: ________________ **Weather:** ________________

Day 13

Date: ____________________ **Weather:** ____________________

Day 14

Date: **Weather:**

Day 15

Date: ______________ **Weather:** ______________

Day 16

Date: ____________ **Weather:** ____________

Day 17

Date: **Weather:**

Day 18

Date: ________________ **Weather:** ________________

Day 19

Date: ____________ **Weather:** ____________

Day 20

Date: ______________ **Weather:** ______________

Day 21

Date: ________________ **Weather:** ________________

Memories of your Trip

Things I will remember from the trip

Favorite Places visited on the Trip

People I Met

Name:
Address:
Tel:
email:

Name:
Address:
Tel:
email:

Name:
Address:
Tel:
email:

Name:
Address:
Tel:
email:

Name:
Address:
Tel:
email:

Name:
Address:
Tel:
email:

Name:
Address:
Tel:
email:

Name:
Address:
Tel:
email:

Name:
Address:
Tel:
email:

Name:
Address:
Tel:
email:

Name:
Address:
Tel:
email:

We hope you enjoyed your trip to Belize

Please leave us a review if you found this Journal useful

Check out our useful resources on the next few pages

Clothes & Shoe Sizes

Children's Shoe Sizes

UK	EUROPE	US	Japan
4	20	4½ or 5	12 ½
4 ½	21	5 or 5½	13
5	21 or 22	5½ or 6	13 ½
5 ½	22	6	13½ or 14
6	23	6½ or 7	14 or 14½
6 ½	23 or 24	7 ½	14½ or 15
7	24	7½ or 8	15
7 ½	25	8 or 9	15 ½
8	25 or 26	8½ or 9	16
8 ½	26	9½	16 ½
9	27	9½ or 10	16 ½ or 17
10	28	10½ or 11	17 ½
10½ or 11	29	11½ or 12	18
11 ½	30	12½	18 or 18 ½
12	31	13	19 or 19 ½
12 ½	31	13 or 13½	19 ½ or 20
13	32	1	20
13 ½	32 ½	1 ½	20 ½
1	33	1½ or 2	21
2	34	2½ or 3	22

Children's Clothing Sizes

UK	EUROPE	US	Australia
12m	80cm	12-18m	12m
18m	80-86cm	18-24m	18m
24m	86-92cm	23-24m	2
2-3	92-98cm	2T	3
3-4	98-104cm	4T	4
3-5	104-110cm	5	5
5-6	110-116cm	6	6
6-7	116-122cm	6X-7	7
7-8	122-128cm	7 to 8	8
8-9	128-134cm	9 to 10	9
9-10	134-140cm	10	10
10-11	140-146cm	11	11
11-12	146-152cm	14	12

Women's Shoe Sizes

UK	EUROPE	US	Japan
3	35 ½	5	22 ½
3 ½	36	5 ½	23
4	37	6	23
4 ½	37 ½	6 ½	23 ½
5	38	7	24
5 ½	39	7 ½	24
6	39 ½	8	24 ½
6 ½	40	8 ½	25
7	41	9 ½	25 ½
7 ½	41 ½	10	26
8	42	10 ½	26 ½

Women's Clothes Sizes

UK	US	Japan	France / Spain	Germany	Belize	Australia
6/8	6	7-9	36	34	40	8
10	8	9-11	38	36	42	10
12	10	11-13	40	38	44	12
14	12	13-15	42	39	46	14
16	14	15-17	44	40	48	16
18	16	17-19	46	42	50	18
20	18	19-21	48	44	52	20

Men's Shoe Sizes

UK	EUROPE	US	Japan
6	38 ½	6 ½	24 ½
6 ½	39	7	25
7	40	7 ½	25 ½
7 ½	41	8	26
8	42	8 ½	27 ½
8 ½	43	9	27 ½
9	43 ½	9 ½	28
9 ½	44	10	28 ½
10	44	10 ½	28 ½
10 ½	44 ½	11	29
11	45	12	29 ½

Men's Suit / Coat / Sweater Sizes

UK / US / Aus	EU / Japan	General
32	42	Small
34	44	Small
36	46	Small
38	48	Medium
40	50	Large
42	52	Large
44	54	Extra Large
46	56	Extra Large

Men's Pants / Trouser Sizes (Waist)

UK / US	Europe
32	81 cm
34	86 cm
36	91 cm
38	97 cm
40	102 cm
42	107 cm

Common Translations

English	French	Spanish	Italian
Hello	Bonjour	Hola	Ciao
Goodbye	Au revoir	Adiós	Arrivederci
Yes	Oui	Sí	Si
No	Non	No	No
Please	S'il-vous-plaît	Por favor	Per favore
Thank you	Merci	Gracias	Grazie
Excuse me	Excusez-moi	Perdón	Mi scusi
How much	Combien	Cuánto	Quanto
My name is	Mon nom est	Mi nombre es	Io mi chiamo
Where is	Où est	Dónde está	Dov'è
The bank	La banque	El banco	La banca
The toilet	Les toilettes	El baño	Il bagno

German	Japanese	Mandarin	Hindi
Hallo	Kon'nichiwa	Ni hao	Namaste
Auf Wiedersehen	Sayonara	Zaijian	Alavida
Ja	Hai	Shi de	Ham
Nein	Ie	Meiyou	Nahim
Bitte	Onegaishimasu	Qing	Krpaya
Vielen Dank	Arigato	Xiexie	Dhan'yavada
Entschuldigung	Sumimasen	Duoshao	Mujhe mapha karem
Wie viel	Ikura	Wo de mingzi shi	Kitana
Mein Name ist	Watashinonamaeha	Nali	Mera nama hai
Wo ist	Doko ni aru	Yinhang	Kaham hai
Die Bank	Ginko	Yinhang	Bainka
Die Toilette	Toire	Cesuo	Saucalaya

Notes:

Made in United States
Orlando, FL
17 April 2025

60606638R00077